DESIGNING THE FUTURE

Published by Creative Education
123 South Broad Street, Mankato, Minnesota 56001
Creative Education is an imprint of The Creative Company

Designed by Stephanie Blumenthal

Photographs by Richard Nowitz

Library of Congress Cataloging-in-Publication Data

Chapman, Lynne F. (Lynne Ferguson)
Egyptian Pyramids / by Lynne Ferguson Chapman
p. cm. — (Designing the future)
Includes index
Summary: Examines the history, building, structure,
and purpose of the Egyptian pyramids.
ISBN 0-88682-717-5
1. Pyramids—Egypt—Juvenile literature. [1. Pyramids—Egypt.
2. Egypt—Antiquities.] I. Title. II. Series.
DT63.C52   1999
726'.8'0932—dc21   98-30295

First Edition

2 4 6 8 9 7 5 3 1

EGYPTIAN PYRAMIDS

LYNNE FERGUSON CHAPMAN

CREATIVE EDUCATION

A stone cutter watched with his fellow laborers as the rock he had carved was moved into place at the base of a pyramid. This was to be the tomb of King Mycerinus, and it would be constructed with the largest stones ever used on a pyramid. Thousands of laborers would work for many years to complete this pyramid. To be part of such an enormous undertaking gave the stone cutter a sense of great pride.

The Arabs called them the "Mountains of Pharaoh," after the Egyptian kings who were buried

Cheops Pyramid (center), Pyramids of Giza

Hieroglyphics on wall

Egypt itself, pyramids are the world's oldest stone buildings and among the largest structures ever built. It is only during the last two centuries that people have cracked the code of the ancient Egyptian picture writing known as hieroglyphics and begun to understand how and why the pyramids were built.

Building began on the first pyramid only

deep within their massive stone walls; we know them simply as the pyramids. Together they are one of the Seven Wonders of the Ancient World. Awesome and mysterious, pyramids have towered over the Egyptian desert for more than 4,500 years. Although the largest and best-built of these structures stand on the Giza Plateau near Egypt's modern-day capital, Cairo, there are many more rising above the landscape along the mighty Nile River. Almost as ancient as the nation of

Reproduction of Rosetta Stone

Step Pyramid of Zoser, Saqqâra

decades after a king named Menes, in 2686 B.C., united two kingdoms in North Africa's Nile River valley. Compared to the many civilizations that have existed since, ancient Egypt lasted an incredibly long time. Egyptian power finally began to fade when the Greeks, under the leadership of Alexander the Great, seized control of the country in 332 B.C., followed by the Romans about 300 years later.

Today, when we think of the ancient Egyptians, tombs and mummies often come to mind. The

Wall paintings at Great Sphinx

Egyptians were certainly preoccupied with death and the afterlife, but the great demands of everyday life must have pushed those concerns aside much of the time. The average Egyptian was a hardworking peasant farmer who raised herd animals or grew crops. The pharaoh was the head of the ruling family in Egypt, but he was much more than just a king; people thought he was a god. His subjects thought he controlled the sunrise and the Nile River's annual flood. The Egyptians believed that they must obey his every command, and in return he would ensure that their land prospered.

If people's good deeds outweighed their bad ones, the Egyptians believed their spirits would live on after death. But certain precautions had to be taken to

The Step Pyramid at Saqqāra, the world's oldest stone building, contains more than a million tons (907,000 metric tons) of solid rock.

ensure that the afterlife lasted forever. The spirit, or ka, had to be able to recognize the body after death, so the Egyptians preserved the deceased in a process called mummification, which involved wrapping the body in many layers of bandages before being placed in a coffin. In the case of a pharaoh, the coffin was then placed in a magnificent tomb designed to last forever. In the early years of the Old Kingdom,

Wall painting depicts mourners at the Tombs of Nobles

Statues of Ramses II

pharaohs began to build huge pyramids that housed such tombs. For the next several centuries, pyramid building would be a way of life in Egypt.

The earliest tombs for pharaohs were squat rectangular structures called mastabas built of sun-dried mud bricks. Then, in about 2646 B.C., a great architect named Imhotep was ordered to design a tomb for the pharaoh Zoser at Saqqâra. Imhotep didn't think a mud-brick mastaba would last long enough to be a suitable burial place for a king, so he used blocks of stone instead. He was probably the first person ever to construct a building from cut stone. But the architect was still not satisfied. So he built another, smaller mastaba on top of the first one, and then another on top of that . . . and when he

The pharaoh Ramses II built an amazing temple at Abu Simbel. Engineers designed it so that the sun's rays would pierce the innermost chamber only twice per year, illuminating the statues of the gods inside.

was through, he had built the world's first step pyramid. A few generations after Imhotep, architects began to build stone pyramids which rose smoothly upward.

An Egyptian pharaoh might order an architect to design a burial place, but the project could go no further than plans without a large labor force.

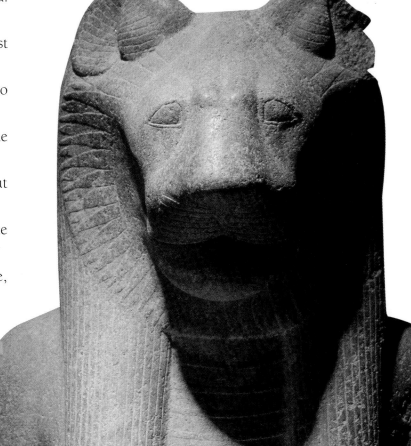

Powerful Goddess Sakhmet of Memphis

Camels are strong desert animals

Historians are divided as to how many workers were required to build the pyramids. Some suggest as many as 80,000 men, while others think crews were more likely to number 4,000 to 8,000 men. Craftsmen such as stone cutters, stonemasons, surveyors, carpenters, and mortar makers would do the skilled labor, and the peasants, who were not able to work in the fields because the land lay under water, would haul the massive blocks of stone. Building a pyramid would put food in the peasants' stomachs during these lean months. The work would also ensure the protection of Egypt, because the pharaoh would be able to unite with the gods after death.

Although the pyramid built for Khufu is known as the Great Pyramid, the pyramid built for his son Khafre looks bigger because it stands on higher ground and still has some of its limestone casing.

Tuthmosis III with Atef crown at Luxor Museum

Before the long building process could begin, the pharaoh and his architect had to settle on a site to the west of the Nile. Priests, who were also astronomers, would then study the stars to work out the correct alignment of the structure. The pyramid's sides must face exactly north, south, east, and west. Workers could then clear the site, level it, and mark out the square base on the ground. Measurements had to be precise or the walls of the pyramid might one day collapse. The Bent Pyramid at Dashur, for example, was half-built when the architects decided that the angle of the walls was too steep. The sides, therefore, slope more gently at the bottom.

Workers sometimes traveled great distances to

> The burial chamber for the pharaoh inside the Great Pyramid is as large as a modern two-story house: 32 feet (10 m) by 16 feet (5 m) and 20 feet (6 m) high.

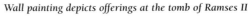
Wall painting depicts offerings at the tomb of Ramses II

Nile River

quarry the hundreds of thousands of limestone blocks needed for the walls of the pyramid and the harder granite needed for roofing slabs and pillars. An average block weighed 2.5 tons (2.3 t), about as much as three adult camels. The largest stone block in any Egyptian pyramid, used for the tomb of King Mycerinus, weighed approximately 285 tons (260 t)! Yet the laborers had only primitive tools. They used hammers and chisels for cutting and shaping the blocks; wooden wedges which, when soaked with water, would swell and split the blocks apart; and ropes, levers, wooden sleds, and rollers for hauling the stone. They had no hoists, pulleys, or wheeled vehicles. As they did for so many things, the Egyptians depended on the Nile to help them move the massive blocks great distances. After the blocks were dragged

to the side of the river they were loaded onto barges and floated to the building site.

As the blocks of stone arrived at the site, workers began to maneuver them into place; as many as 30,000 blocks might be needed just for the pyramid's bottom layer. When laborers completed the first level, they worked on the second, and so on, each level smaller than the one before. As the walls gradually rose higher, the workers built long ramps of earth to enable them to drag the stone blocks up to the correct height.

Giza Pyramids at sunset

As the walls went up, laborers had to leave gaps for the burial chamber and the long passageway leading to it; this would be easier than cutting through the stone later. The massive stone sarcophagus that would eventually contain the pharaoh's mummy within its coffin would have been placed in the burial chamber already, because it would not fit down the narrow passageway later. In most pyramids there was only one chamber, with perhaps two or three antechambers, but the Great Pyramid at Giza, the largest in the world, contains three main chambers. (The Great Pyramid was built for the pharaoh Khufu, also commonly known by his Greek name of Cheops.)

The greatest temple ever built is at Karnak in Egypt. Generations of New Kingdom pharaohs added on to the structure until it was big enough to hold a dozen European cathedrals.

Tutankhamen tomb at Valley of the Kings

Most pyramids took more than 20 years to build. The biggest ones consist of more than 100 layers, and even after the builders completed the last level they were far from finished. Their next job was moving the capstone, the huge granite stone which gave the pyramid its point, into place. In most cases the pharaoh himself probably attended the placement ceremony, during which priests burned incense and made numerous prayers and offerings to the gods to ensure their cooperation.

Working from the top of the pyramid down, the builders then began to cover the entire structure with hundreds of casing blocks of a special high-quality limestone, which would later be rubbed smooth with polishing stones. When the pyramid was new, these blocks were a gleaming white that

Akhenaten was also known as Amenhotep IV

Kom Ombo Temple

must have looked dazzling in the desert sun. Very little of the casing remains on pyramids today, because most of the blocks were stolen and used in building parts of the city of Cairo, including a great 16th-century mosque.

Even when the pyramid itself was finished, more building work remained. A pyramid did not stand alone by the side of the Nile; each one was part of a larger complex. On the east side of the pyramid,

P R E S E R V A T I O N

In 1954 archaeologists discovered a pit near the Great Pyramid containing an enormous boat that had belonged to the pharaoh Khufu. Although dismantled into more than 1,200 pieces, it was so well preserved that it could be rebuilt.

Abu Simbel, Great Temple of Ramses II

Face of the Great Sphinx

facing the river, stood the mortuary temple. This was the place where, after the pharaoh's death, priests would make offerings every day to his ka. A long covered passage called the causeway led down to the riverbank where another temple, called the valley temple, stood. The pharaoh's body would be brought here to be mummified. In addition to these structures, many pyramid complexes included a smaller pyramid for the queen as well as numerous mastabas for other relatives or favored members of the court. A deep pit was sometimes dug alongside a pyramid to contain a boat for the pharaoh to use in the afterlife. From the earliest years of pyramid building, the treasures included

Debate continues over the age of the Sphinx—and whether it predates the Giza pyramids. Evidence of water erosion on the Sphinx's face have some researchers believing that the monument dates as far back as 10500 B.C. Other theories suggest only 7000 B.C. or 5000 B.C.

inside the tombs of the pharaohs were a great temptation to thieves. Every pyramid in Egypt was broken into and robbed at one time or another.

During the Middle Kingdom (approximately 2133 to 1786 B.C.), many pharaohs had not ordered pyramids built. Those who had, usually built small ones, sometimes with only a facing of limestone over rubble and mud brick.

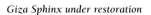

Giza Sphinx under restoration

Interior of temple of Abu Simbel

This was partly because Egypt was not as prosperous during the Middle Kingdom. By the time of the New Kingdom (approximately 1567 to 1085 B.C.), the Egyptians had concluded that pyramids did not make good burial places for pharaohs; they were too obvious and easily accessible. But Egypt was at its most powerful, and pharaohs could once again afford impressive tombs.

The Egyptians carved these tombs out of the rocky hillsides in a place that came to be known as the Valley of the Kings, near the city of Thebes in the south and far from the great pyramids of the Old Kingdom. Although the location of this site was a closely guarded secret, thieves still despoiled most of the tombs. In 1922, however, the archaeologist Howard Carter discovered one that had been un-

Wall carvings at Abu Simbel

touched, that of the pharaoh Tutankhamen. When his team finally broke into the tomb, Carter was "struck dumb with amazement." The chamber before him was filled with "strange animals, statues and gold—everywhere the glint of gold." The tomb contained magnificent jewelry, furniture, and other possessions. The king's mummy, with a gold death mask over its head, lay inside a solid gold coffin.

If Tutankhamen, a king who died when he was only 17 and who had not been particularly accomplished or well-known, had been buried with such riches, even greater treasures must have been stolen over the centuries from the

Other ancient peoples built pyramid-shaped structures for religious purposes. The broadly stepped pyramids known as ziggurats, built by the Mesopotamians, might have been the inspiration for the Tower of Babel.

Tomb of Ramses IV (above); funeral mask of King Tutankhamen (below)

tombs of some of Egypt's greatest pharaohs.

After two and a half centuries of diligent excavation and scholarship in Egypt, we now have answers to many of our questions about the pyramids. However, many other lingering mysteries continue to intrigue people all over the world.

Although modern people can understand the basic process of building a pyramid, we have difficulty comprehending the scale on which it was done. The Great Pyramid is 481 feet (146 meters) high and contains 2.3 million blocks of stone. That's enough to build a low wall

Pyramids at Giza

around Earth! The pyramid was also built with uncanny precision: the difference between the longest side and the shortest side is only eight inches (20 cm), the base is almost perfectly flat, and the casing stones on the outside were positioned so exactly that not even a hair can be pushed between the joints.

Many of the interiors of pyramids were decorated to make the pharaoh comfortable in his afterlife. A fine example is the magnificent mortuary temple of King Sahure (about 2474 B.C.) where thousands of stars cover the ceiling in the cloister around the court.

How these ancient people, with their simple tools, performed such astonishing building feats have baffled engineers and architects for centuries. Today, technology is helping to answer some questions about the pyramids. To teach us more about the ancient Egyptians, archaeologists can use medical scanners and computer graphics

Luxor Temple in Egypt

to recreate the faces of mummies.

To further explore the pyramids, they can send tiny robots inside to travel along the shafts that are too narrow for archaeologists to crawl through. These robots can transmit pictures taken with video cameras. In recent years, both a French team and a Japanese team claimed to have evidence of additional chambers within the Great Pyramid that have never been opened. Such a find would be the greatest in

DECORATION

The color that decorates the statue of King Sesotris has lasted nearly 4000 years.

Statues of Ramses II, Luxor Temple

Louvre Museum in France (above); Thutmose III (opposite)

Egypt since the discovery of Tutankhamen's tomb.

Learning more about the ancient Egyptians can only heighten our sense of awe at what they accomplished. The pharaohs built the pyramids to assure their immortality, and, in a sense, immortality is exactly what they achieved. The pyramids are not just great wonders of the ancient world—they are among the greatest wonders in the history of humankind. As long as they remain standing, the civilization of ancient Egypt will be remembered.

INDEX

Pyramids at Giza in Egypt